# Apple Treats
### *from*
## Amish Country

**With Art by Amish Children**

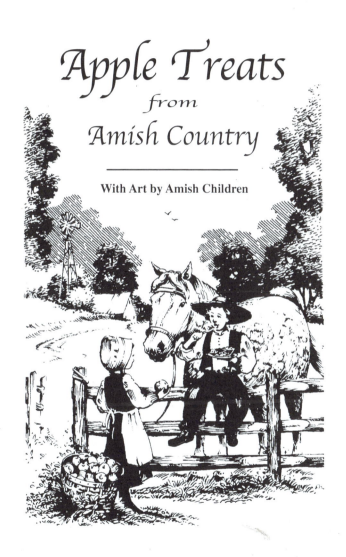

**By Adrienne Lund**

## A WORD OF THANKS

I would like to express my appreciation to the Amish home-makers who generously shared their favorite apple recipes to create this book.

Thanks also to Andrew, David and Mervin Miller who contributed their drawings of Amish life.

## THE ARTISTS

Many thanks to Wayne Troyer of Troyer Arts, Millersburg, Ohio for the beautiful cover art. His excellent work is deeply appreciated.

Sincere appreciation to Walter Pitts for producing the apple graphics for the interior of the book.

This book is dedicated to Aja Leland, Heather Lund, and Austin Wade, the apples of my eye.

# _BREADS, ROLLS, ETC!_

 ## _Delicious Apple Rolls_

3 Tbsp. Shortening
1/2 C Milk
2 C Flour
4 Apples, cut fine

2 Tbsp. Sugar
1 Egg, Beaten
4 tsp. Baking Powder

Mix flour and shortening into crumbles. Add milk and egg.
Mix to a dough and roll 1/2 in. thick. Spread with butter and
add apples. Then sprinkle with cinnamon. Roll up, and cut in
1 in. slices. Pour over syrup and bake at 375° until done.

## _Syrup_

Mix well:

2 C Brown Sugar                    1/2 C Hot Water

_Sarah Miller_
_Jeromesville, Ohio_

# _Apple Doughnuts_

2 Eggs
3 tsp. Baking Powder
1 1/2 tsp. Salt
3 or 4 Apples, peeled
1 C Milk, add more if needed

2 C Sugar
1 tsp. Nutmeg
1 Tbsp. Melted Shortening
3 C Sifted Flour (or more)

Continued

1

Beat eggs until light. Add sugar and milk. Sift dry ingredients, and add to egg mixture. Add melted shortening and enough flour to make a soft dough. Roll out to 1/4 in. thickness. Put layer of diced apples on, cover with another layer of dough. Cut out with cutter. Fry in deep fat.

*Sarah Miller*
*Jeromesville, Ohio*

# *Applesauce Muffins*

1 C Flour
1 C Whole Wheat Flour
2 tsp. Cinnamon
1/4 C Sugar
1/2 tsp. Cloves

1 tsp. Baking Soda
1/2 C Butter
1 1/2 C Applesauce
1/2 C Raisins

Sift dry ingredients together. Cream butter, applesauce and sugar together. Add raisins. Combine the two. Pour into greased muffin tin. Bake at 350° for 20 to 25 min.

*Mrs. David Miller*
*Applecreek, Ohio*

# *Apple-Cinnamon Waffles*

2 C Whole Wheat Flour
4 tsp. Baking Powder
3 tsp. Cinnamon
2 C. Grated, Peeled Apples
   (about 2 apples)

6 Tbsp. Vegetable Oil
2 C Milk
2 Eggs, Separated

Continued

2

Preheat waffle iron on high. Sift flour, baking powder, and cinnamon together. Beat yolks with oil until blended. Add milk and apple. Add dry ingredients and mix until moistened. Beat egg whites until stiff and fold into batter. Drop on preheated, oiled waffle iron and bake until browned, about 6 to 8 minutes. Excess waffles can be frozen in plastic bags and reheated in toaster. Makes 4 (9 in.) square waffles.

*Mrs. David Miller*
*Applecreek, Ohio*

# *Apple Rolls*

Sift together 2 C flour, 3 tsp. Baking Powder, 1/2 tsp. salt, 2 Tbsp. Sugar. blend into 3 Tbsp. Butter, add 1 well Beaten Egg and 3/8 C Milk, blend well. Roll dough out on floured board about 1 in. thick.

Peel, core and chop fine 4 med. apples and arrange on dough. Sprinkle apples with 4 Tbsp. Sugar and 3/4 tsp. Cinnamon. Dot with 1 Tbsp. Butter. Roll as for jelly roll. Mix together 1 1/2 C Brown Sugar and 1/4 C Hot Water. Pour into 10 x 16 in. pan. Cut rolls in 1/2 in. slices and lay in syrup. Bake in moderate oven 1/2 hour at 350° or until golden brown.

*Laura Brenneman*
*Morley, Michigan*

*Blessed are those who see the hand of God in the haphazard, inexplicable and senseless circumstances of life.*

# *Apple Bread*

1/2 C Shortening
1 C Sugar
2 Eggs
2 C Flour
1 tsp. Salt

1 tsp. Soda
1 tsp. Baking Powder
1 tsp. Vanilla
2 Tbsp. Buttermilk
2 C Peeled, Sliced Apples

Cream shortening and sugar until light and fluffy. Add eggs and beat well. Combine flour, salt and baking powder and add soda; add to creamed mixture and beat well. Stir in butter, milk, cinnamon, vanilla and apples. Spoon batter into a greased 8 1/2 x 4 1/2 x 2 1/2 in. loaf pan. Bake at 350° for 1 hour.

*Mrs. David Miller*
*Applecreek, Ohio*

# *Apple Bread*

2 C Sugar
1 C Oil or Oleo
3 C Flour
1 tsp. Soda
1 tsp. Salt

1 tsp. Cinnamon
3 Eggs
2 tsp. Vanilla
3 C Chopped Apples
1 C Chopped Nuts

Mix oil or oleo and sugar. Add flour, soda, salt and cinnamon; beat all together well, then add eggs and beat again. Add chopped apples and nuts. Pour into 2 greased and floured loaf pans and sprinkle with sugar. Bake at 325° for 1 hour.

*Mrs. Orie Detweiler*
*Inola, Oklahoma*

 *Apple Dip*

1 8 oz. Package Cream Cheese
1 Small Jar Marshmallow Creme
Thin with Pineapple Juice

Mix together till smooth. Core and slice apples. Dip-n-Eat! Delicious!!

Can also dip bananas, strawberries, oranges, pineapple & grapes.

*Carol Coblentz*
*Grandin, Missouri*

# *Apple Danish*
## *Pastry:*

3 C Flour
1 C Shortening
1/2 C Milk

1/2 tsp. Salt
1 Egg Yolk

## *Filling:*

6 C Sliced Peeled Apples
1/4 C Butter - Melted
1 tsp. Cinnamon

1/2 C Sugar
2 Tbsp. Flour

Continued

# Glaze:

1 Egg White, Lightly Beaten          1/2 C Confectioners' Sugar
2-3 tsp. Water

In a mixing bowl, combine flour and salt; cut in shortening
until mixture resembles coarse crumbs. Combine egg yolk and
milk; add to flour mixture. Stir just until dough clings
together. Divide dough in half. On a lightly floured surface,
roll half of dough into a 15 in. x 10 in. baking pan. Set aside.
In a bowl, toss together filling ingredients; spoon over pastry
in pan. Roll out remaining dough to another 15 in. x 10 in.
rectangle. Place over filling. Brush with egg white. Bake at
375° for 40 minutes or until golden brown. Cool on a wire
rack. Combine the confectioners' sugar and enough water to
achieve a drizzling consistency. Drizzle over warm pastry.
Cut into squares. Serve warm or cold. Delicious!!

*Carol Coblentz*
*Grandin, Missouri*

 ## Apple Rolls

2 C Flour                          2 Tbsp. Sugar
4 C Chopped Apples                 1/2 tsp. Salt
4 tsp. Baking Powder               2 Tbsp. Shortening
1/2 C Milk or enough
    milk to make a soft dough

Mix flour, baking powder and salt. Cream sugar and
shortening; add dry ingredients to creamed mixture,
alternating with milk. Roll this out 1/4 in. thick. Have apples

Continued

cut fine or shredded.  Put apples on dough and roll like jelly roll and cut 1 1/4 in. thick.  Place slices in long pan and pour hot syrup over and bake till apples are soft and brown.

## *Syrup*

1 1/2 C Brown Sugar
Butter - Size of Egg

2 C Water

Bring to boil, pour over rolls.  Bake at 400° for about 25 min.

*Alta C. Schlabach*
*Millersburg, Ohio*

# *Apple Pancakes*

1 1/2 C Flour
1 1/2 tsp. Baking Powder
3/4 tsp. Salt
1 Tbsp. Sugar

1 Egg Beaten
1 C Milk
2 C Apples, Finely Chopped

Combine dry ingredients.  Add egg, milk and butter.  Stir until smooth.  Fold in apples and fry until golden brown.

*Edith Miller*
*Kalona, Iowa*

# *Red Apple Rings*

Slice cored apples into 1/2 in. thick rings.  Cook until tender in a  syrup made of:

2 C Sugar
1/3 C Red Cinnamon Candies
Few Drops of Red Food Coloring

1 C Water

*Edith Miller*
*Kalona, Iowa*

# COOKIES

## Diced Apple Cookies

4 Eggs
2 C Brown Sugar
1 tsp. Salt
1 C Sour Cream
2 tsp. Vanilla
2 C Chocolate Chips or Nuts

1 C Shortening
2 C White Sugar
3 tsp. Soda
6 C Flour
4 C Apples (Diced)

Cream shortening with sugar. Beat in eggs. Add vanilla. Sift dry ingredients. Mix alternately with sour cream. Last of all fold in apples. Drop by teaspoonfuls on lightly floured cookie sheet. Bake at 350° until light golden brown.

*Ruby Hochstetler*
*Sulivan, Illinois*

8

Home sweet ♡ Home

Andrew Miller
Applecreek, Ohio
Age 9

# Apple Bars

Cream together:

3 Eggs                                    1 C Oil
1 3/4 C Sugar

Add:

2 C Flour                                 1/2 tsp. Salt
1 tsp. Baking Powder                      1 tsp. Cinnamon
1 C Nuts                                  2 C Diced Apples

Mix well and pour into greased 9 x 13 pan.  Bake at 350° to 400° for 30 to 40 min.  Sprinkle with powdered sugar if desired.

*Sarah Miller*
*Jeromesville, Ohio*

# Apple Cookies

2 C Flour                                 1 tsp. Baking Soda
1 1/3 C Brown Sugar                       1/2 tsp. Salt
1 tsp. Cinnamon                           1/4 tsp. Cloves
1 Egg                                     1/2 C Shortening
1/4 C Apple Juice                         1 C Raisins
1 C Walnuts                               1 1/2 C Chopped Fine
                                              Apples

Mix all dry ingredients together, cream sugar and shortening.  Add egg and juice, apples, raisins and walnuts.  Drop by spoonfuls on ungreased baking sheet.  Bake at 400° for 12 to 15 min.

Continued

# Icing

1 1/2 C Powdered Sugar          3 Tbsp. Butter
3 Tbsp. Cream                   3/4 tsp. Vanilla

Mix well.  Spread on warm cookies.  Makes 30 cookies.

*Laura Brenneman*
*Morley, Michigan*

# Fresh Apple Bars

3 Eggs                          1 C Cooking Oil
1 3/4 C White Sugar

Beat above ingredients well, then add the rest:

2 C All Purpose Flour           1/2 tsp. Salt
1/2 tsp. Cinnamon               1 tsp. Soda
2 C Chopped Fine Apples         1 C Chopped Nuts or Raisins

Spread mixture on lightly greased cookie sheet.  This is enough for a 8 x 12 cookie sheet.  Bake at 350° for 30 minutes or until done.

*Mattie Yoder*
*Charm, Ohio*

*A hug is a great gift...one size fits all and it's easy to exchange.*

# *Glazed Apple Cookies*

| | |
|---|---|
| 1/2 C Shortening | 1 1/2 C Packed Brown Sugar |
| 1 tsp. Baking Soda | 1 tsp. Salt |
| 1 tsp. Cinnamon | 1 tsp. Ground Cloves |
| 1/2 tsp. Nutmeg | 1 Egg, Beaten |
| 1 C Finely Chopped Apples | 1 C Chopped Nuts |
| 1 C Raisins | 1/2 C Apple Juice or Milk |
| 2 C Flour | 1 1/2 C Powdered Sugar |
| 1 Tbsp. Butter | 1/4 tsp. Vanilla |
| 1/8 tsp. Salt | 2 1/2 Tbsp. Light Cream |

Beat together shortening, sugar, soda, salt, spices, and egg in large bowl. Stir in apples, nuts, raisins, juice, and half the flour. Mix well. Blend in remaining flour and drop by heaping teaspoons onto greased cookie sheet. Bake at 350° for 10 to 12 mins.

Combine powdered sugar, butter, 1/4 tsp. vanilla, 1/8 tsp. salt, and cream for glaze. Drizzle glaze over cookies while they are still warm.

*Sarah Miller*
*Jeromesville, Ohio*

# Apple Chip Cookies

1/4 C Butter
1 C Brown Sugar
1/2 C Cream
1 Egg
1/2 tsp. Baking Soda
1/2 tsp. Salt

1/4 tsp. Nutmeg
2 C Flour
1 C Pared, Chopped Apples
1/2 C Chocolate or
  Butterscotch Chips
1 C Chopped Nuts

## Glaze

3 Tbsp. Melted Butter
1 tsp. Cinnamon

2 Tbsp. Cream
2 C Confectioners' Sugar

Cream butter and sugar. Beat in cream, egg, soda, salt, nutmeg and flour. Add apples, chips and nuts. Drop by teaspoonfuls onto greased cookie sheet. Bake at 350° 12 to 15 mins. Do not overbake! Glaze: Combine ingredients, spread over cooled cookies.

*Edith Miller*
*Kalona, Iowa*

*Trouble and perplexity drive us to prayer, and prayer driveth away trouble and perplexity.*

# Spicy Apple Squares

2/3 C Butter
1 C Sugar
2 Eggs
1 C Flour
1 tsp. Baking Powder
1 tsp. Cinnamon
1/2 tsp. Soda

1/2 tsp. Nutmeg
1/4 tsp. Cloves (ground)
1 C Diced Apples
3/4 C Rolled Oats
1/2 C Chopped Walnuts
Confectioners' Sugar

Cream together butter and sugar until light and fluffy. Add eggs one at a time, beating well. Sift together flour , baking powder, spices and soda. Gradually add dry ingredients to creamed mixture. Mix well. Stir in apples, oats and nuts. Spread batter into greased 9 x 13 in. pan. Bake at 350° for 25 to 30 min. or until done. Cool in pan on rack. Sprinkle with confectioners' sugar. Makes 15 bars.

*Vernie Schwartz*
*Stanwood, Michigan*

# Applesauce Cookies

1 Pkg. Spice Cake Mix
1 C Raisins
1/2 C Cooking Oil

1/2 C Applesauce
1 Egg

In large mixing bowl, combine cake mix, raisins, cooking oil, applesauce, and egg. Beat for 1 minute. Drop from teaspoon 2 inches apart on ungreased cookie sheet and bake 12 to 15 mins. at 350°. Yield 6 dozen.

*Mrs. Orie Detweiler*
*Inola, Ohio*

# Easy Apple Filled Cookies

1 C Shortening
1/2 C Milk
2 1/4 tsp. Soda
Flour (enough to make a
fairly soft dough)

2 C Brown Sugar
2 tsp. Vanilla
2 1/2 tsp. Cream of Tartar
3 Well Beaten Eggs

Cream sugar and shortening. Add eggs and vanilla. Mix dry ingredients and mix into creamed mixture alternately with milk.

## Filling:

1 C Chopped Apples
1 Tbsp. Cornstarch
1 Tsp. Flour

1 C Water
1 C Brown Sugar

Cook apples, water, cornstarch, brown sugar, and flour together until thick. Set aside to cool.

Put a teaspoon of dough on cookie sheet, flatten out, leaving a little shallow hollow place, then fill up with filling. Put a little dough on top and bake until brown. Makes 2 dozen or more. Bake at 350°

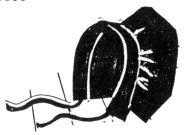

*Lobelville, Tennessee*

# Apple Bars

| | |
|---|---|
| 1 3/4 C White Sugar | 1 C Vegetable Oil |
| 3 Eggs | 2 C All-purpose Flour |
| 1/2 tsp. Salt | 1/2 tsp. Cinnamon |
| 1 tsp. Baking soda | 2 C chopped Apples |

Beat eggs, white sugar, add vegetable oil. Beat well, then add the rest of the ingredients. Bake at 350° for 20-25 min. in a lightly greased (15 1/2 x 10 1/2 x 1) pan. Cool and cut in bars.

Delicious with cream cheese icing!

## Cream Cheese Icing

| | |
|---|---|
| 8 oz. Cream Cheese | 6 Tbsp. Butter - Softened |
| 1 Tbsp. Milk | 1 tsp. Vanilla |
| 3 1/2 C Powdered Sugar | |

Cream together cream cheese, butter, milk and vanilla. Add powdered sugar. Spread on cooled cake.

*Mrs. Roman Hersberger*
*Millersburg, Ohio*

David M. Miller
Applecreek, Ohio
Age 8

# Sugarless Fruit Cookies

1 C Oleo
1 C Bananas
1 3/4 C Unsweetened
  Applesauce
3/4 tsp. Salt
2 C Raisins
2 C Nuts

2 Eggs
1 1/4 C Pineapple (Crushed)
4 1/2 C Flour
4 tsp. Soda
1 tsp. Cinnamon
2 C Dates

Mix and bake by spoonfuls on cookie sheet. Bake at 375° until golden brown. 12 to 15 minutes. ( We make these at the bakery for diabetics.)

*Carol Coblentz*
*Grandin, Missouri*

*Grace is the love that gives, that loves the unlovely
and the unlovable.*

# Apple Oatmeal Cookies

1 1/2 C Quick Oats
3/4 C All Purpose Flour
3/4 C Whole Wheat Flour
1/2 C Brown Sugar
1 tsp. Baking Powder
1/4 tsp. Baking Soda
1/2 tsp. Salt

1 1/2 tsp. Cinnamon
1/2 C Raisins
1 C Chopped, Peeled Apples
1 Egg, Beaten Slightly
1/2 C Honey
1/2 C Oil
1/3 C Milk

Preheat oven to 375°F.

In a medium bowl combine white and whole wheat flour, oats, baking powder, baking soda, salt and cinnamon. Stir to combine. Stir in raisins and apples. In a large bowl, combine eggs, honey, oil and milk. Stir in dry ingredients. Mix to form a smooth batter. Drop rounded teaspoonfuls onto ungreased baking sheets, leaving 2 in. between each. Dip fingers in water and press dough down to about 1 1/2 in diameter. Bake 10 to 12 minutes or until lightly golden. Makes 3 dozen cookies.

*Sadie Brenneman*
*Morley Michigan*

*Any concern too small to be turned into a prayer is too small to be made into a burden.*

# DESSERTS!

## Spiced Apple Dessert

4 Large Apples (cube or slice)
1 C Brown Sugar
1 C Flour
1/2 tsp. Soda
1 tsp. Cinnamon
2 Eggs, Beaten

1/2 tsp. Baking Powder
1 tsp. Nutmeg
1 tsp. Cloves
1/2 tsp. Salt
4 Tbsp. Butter

Put dry ingredients together then add apples, eggs and butter. Bake 45 minutes at 350° in a buttered 9 x 9 in. baking pan or dish.

Eat with milk and sugar when cooled.

*Lobelville, Tennessee*

## Chocolate Chip Applesauce Cake

1/2 C Shortening
1 1/2 C Sugar
2 Eggs
2 C Applesauce
1 tsp. Vanilla
2 C Flour
1/2 C Nuts

1/2 tsp. Cinnamon
1 tsp. Salt
1 1/2 tsp. Soda
3 Tbsp. Cocoa
2 Tbsp. Sugar
1 C Chocolate Chips

Continued

Andrew M. Miller
Applecreek, Ohio
Age 9

Beat shortening, sugar and eggs. Alternately add dry ingredients, applesauce and vanilla. Mix well. Pour in greased and floured 9 x 13 in. cake pan and sprinkle 2 tablespoons sugar and nuts and chocolate chips on top. Bake at 350° for 45 minutes.

*Mrs. Orie Detweiler*
*Inola, Oklahoma*

 # Steamed Apple Pudding

1 1/2 C Sifted All-purpose Flour
1/4 C Soft Butter or Margarine
1 tsp. Baking Soda
1/2 tsp. Cinnamon
1/2 tsp. Nutmeg
1/4 tsp. Cloves
1/2 C Dark Raisins

1 C Sugar
2 Eggs, Well Beaten
4 Pared Medium Apples, shredded (2 1/2 C)
Light Cream

Grease well a 1 1/2 qt. heat-proof bowl. Into small bowl, sift flour with baking soda, salt and spices and set aside. In large bowl with wooden spoon beat butter, sugar and eggs until mixture is smooth and light. Stir in apples and raisins. Stir flour mixture into the fruit mixture, mixing well and turn into greased bowl. Cover surface of pudding with double thickness of waxed paper. Cover top of bowl completely with foil and tie edge securely with twine. Place bowl on trivet in large kettle. Pour boiling water around bowl to come halfway up side. Cover kettle and bring to boiling. Reduce heat and boil gently for two hours. Serve with whipped cream.

*Mrs. Eileen Miller*
*Applecreek, Ohio*

# *Apple Goodie*

Base:

1 1/2 C Sugar
2 Tbsp. Flour
Pinch Salt

1 tsp. Cinnamon
1 1/2 Qt. Sliced Apples

Mix sugar, flour, salt and cinnamon.  Add to apples and mix.
Put in bottom of greased cake pan.

Topping:

1 C Oatmeal
1 C Brown Sugar
1 C Flour

1/4 tsp. Soda
1/3 tsp. Baking Powder
2/3 C Butter

Mix together until crumbly and place evenly on top of apples
and pat firmly.  Bake until brown and crust is formed.  Serve
with milk or cream.

*Mrs. Ervin E. Miller*

*Contentment does not come to those who's means are great but to
those who's needs are small.*

23

# Apple Cake

2 C Apples, Sliced
1/4 C Cooking Oil
1 C Flour
1 tsp. Flour
1 tsp. Cinnamon

1 C Sugar
1 Egg
1 tsp. Soda
1/4 tsp. Salt
1 tsp. Vanilla

Mix apples and sugar in bowl and let stand 10 minutes. Add
oil and egg and mix well. Add dry ingredients and stir in
vanilla. Bake in 8 in. or 9 in. cake pan. Bake at 350° for 45 to 50
minutes. About halfway through baking time cake may be
sprinkled with mixture of: 2 Tbsp. Sugar and 1 tsp. cinnamon.
May be served with or without Cool Whip, as desired.

*Mrs. Rebecca Miller*

# Baked Apples

10 Apples - peeled and halved or quartered. Combine in
saucepan:
1/4 C Melted Butter
1 C Brown Sugar

2 Tbsp. Flour
Add 1 C Water

Cook - Stirring constantly until mixture is caramelized to light
brown. Add 1 cup water. Bring to a boil. Continue boiling
until thick, pour over apples in a baking pan and bake at 350°
until apples are still firm but tender. If desired place
marshmallow in center of each apple. Serve with whipped
topping.

*Mattie Yoder*
*Charm, Ohio*

Andrew Miller
Applecreek, Ohio
Age 9

# Caramel Dip for Apples

1 - 8 oz. pkg. Cream Cheese      1 tsp. Vanilla
1/2 C plus 2 Tbsp. Brown Sugar

Beat all ingredients together and refrigerate. Serve with apple slices.

*Edith Miller*
*Kalona, Iowa*

# Apple Fritters

1 C Flour                 1/2 C Milk
2 Tbsp. Sugar            1 Egg
1 1/2 tsp. Baking Powder    1 C Shredded Apples
1/2 tsp. Salt

Mix like a cake batter and drop by teaspoonful in hot oil in a large skillet. Temperature of 375°. Drain in colander. Roll in sugar and serve immediately.

*Edith Miller*
*Kalona, Iowa*

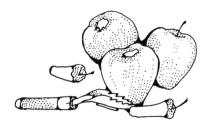

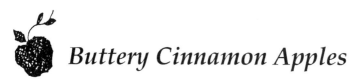

# Buttery Cinnamon Apples

1/3 C Butter
2 Tbsp. Brown Sugar
1/2 tsp. Cinnamon
3 Cooking Apples - peeled and sliced

1/2 C White Sugar
2 Tbsp. Corn Starch
1 1/2 C Water

In medium saucepan melt butter. Stir in sugar, cornstarch and cinnamon. Blend in water. Add sliced apples. Cook over medium heat till boiling. Stir occasionally. Simmer till apples are fork tender and sauce is thick (12 to 20 minutes).

Delicious! Serve on pancakes! Can also add scoop of vanilla ice cream on top yet!

*Mrs. Roman Hershberger*
*Millersburg, Ohio*

# Apple Fritters

1 C Flour
1 Egg
5 or 6 Apples
1 1/2 tsp. Baking Powder

2 Tbsp. Sugar
1/2 C Milk
1/2 tsp. Salt

Core and peel apples. Slice and put in batter. Drop by spoonful in 1 in. fat or oil in frying pan. Drain on paper towel. Sprinkle with powdered sugar or eat with syrup. Jab with fork when frying to test if apples are soft. Be sure fat or oil is hot before dropping batter in.

*Laura Brenneman*
*Morley, Michigan*

# Apple Torte

2 C Peeled, Chopped Apples
1 C Chopped Walnuts
1 C Flour
1 C Sugar
1 tsp. Vanilla

1 tsp. Soda
1/2 tsp. Salt
1 Egg
3 Tbsp. Butter - Soft

Cream sugar and shortening. Beat in egg and vanilla. Mix in dry ingredients. Mix all together and pour into 9 x 9 in pan. Bake at 350° until done. Serve with whipped cream.

*Sarah Miller*
*Jeromesville, Ohio*

# Roman Apple Cake

Beat until creamy:
1 C Sugar
1/4 tsp. Salt
1 Egg
1 tsp. Vanilla
1/4 tsp. Baking Powder

1 1/2 C Flour
1 tsp. Soda
1/2 C Milk
1/2 C Shortening

Cream sugar and shortening. Beat in egg and vanilla. Mix dry ingredients and beat into creamed mixture with milk.
Add: 2 C Chopped Raw Apples  - Mix well and pour into 9 x 13 in. pan.

# Topping

1 Tbsp. Melted Butter
1/2 C Nuts - Chopped
2 Tbsp. Flour

1/2 C Brown Sugar
2 tsp. Cinnamon

Sprinkle on batter and bake at 350° for 35 to 40 minutes.

*Carol Coblentz*
*Grandin, Missouri*

# Apple Crunch

Crumb Ingredients:

1 C Flour
1 tsp. Cinnamon
1/2 C Butter

1 C Brown Sugar
3/4 C Rolled Oats

4 C Peeled, Sliced Apples

Syrup:
1 C Sugar
2 Tbsp. Corn Starch

1 C Water
1 tsp. Vanilla

Mix crumb ingredients until crumbly. Press half of mixture in bottom of pan. Layer apples over crumbs. Boil syrup ingredients and pour over apples. Top with remaining crumbs and bake at 350° for 1 hour.

*Mattie Yoder*
*Charm, Ohio*

# Apple Crisp Dessert

1 C Brown Sugar (packed)
1 C Flour
1 C Oatmeal
1/2 to 1/4 C Sugar
1 tsp. Cinnamon
1/4 tsp. Nutmeg

4 C Sliced Apples
2 Tbsp. Lemon Juice
3/4 C Butter
1/4 C Chopped Walnuts
1/2 tsp. Salt
Whipped Cream or Milk

Combine brown sugar, flour, oatmeal, butter, nuts and salt. Mix together with fork until crumbly. Spread 1/2 of this mixture into 12 x 8 in. baking dish. Arrange apple slices over crumbs. Sprinkle with lemon juice, if apples are not tart, then sprinkle them with sugar cinnamon mixture (amount of sugar depends on tartness of apples). Cover with remaining crumbs. Serve with whipped cream or milk. Bake at 350° for 30 min.

David M. Miller
Applecreek, Ohio
Age 8

# French Apple Pie

2/3 C Sugar
1 tsp. Cinnamon
2 Tbsp. Flour (rounded)

4 C Sliced Apples
Pinch of Salt

Topping:

1/2 C Soft Butter
1/2 C Brown Sugar

1 C Flour

Mix sugar, cinnamon, flour, and salt with apples. Put in unbaked pie shell. Mix topping and put on top. Bake at 300° for 45 minutes. Check, then turn up to 400° until brown.

*Mrs. Orie Detweiler*
*Inola, Oklahoma*

# Apple Bread

3 C Flour
2 C Sugar
1 C Mayonnaise
1/3 C Milk
2 Eggs
More ingredients in directions.

1 tsp. Soda
1 1/2 tsp. Cinnamon
1/2 tsp. Nutmeg
1/4 tsp. Cloves
Dash of Salt

Combine sugar, mayonnaise and eggs. Mix in dry ingredients alternately with milk. Beat for two minutes; stir in 1 cup raisins, 3 cups chopped apples, 3 cups pecans (chopped).

Pour into lightly greased and floured loaf pan. Bake at 350° for 1 hour.

*Lobelville, Tennessee*

31

# Apple Crisp

4 C Finely Cut Apples
1 C Flour
1 Egg, Beaten
3/4 C White Sugar

1/4 tsp. Nutmeg
1/2 C Butter or Margarine
1 C Brown Sugar
1/2 C Nuts (Optional)

Mix apples, egg, sugar and nutmeg together. Place in lightly buttered glass baking dish.

Combine butter, flour and brown sugar and mix to crumbly consistency. Pack over apple mixture. Bake in 375° oven for 30 minutes. Serve with sweetened milk or whipped cream.

*Lobelville, Tennessee*

# Coconut Apple Pie

1 C Sugar
3/4 Qt Apples
  (Peeled and Diced)

2 Tbsp. Flour
1 tsp. Cinnamon
more ingredients in
  directions

Pour into pie pan. Bake 30 minutes at 375°. Then top with the following: 1 Egg, Beaten until fluffy, stir in 1/3 cup sugar, 1/4 cup milk, 2 cups coconut, 1/8 tsp. salt. Bake at 375° for 25 to 30 minutes. Put aluminum foil over top of pie for the first 30 minutes.

*Laura Brenneman*
*Morley, Michigan*

# Apple Cream Pie

3 C Finely Cut Apples
1 C Brown Sugar
2/3 C Cream

1/4 tsp. Salt
1 Rounded Tbsp. Flour

Mix together and put in unbaked pie shell. Sprinkle top with cinnamon. Bake in a hot oven 450° for 15 minutes. Then reduce heat to 325° and bake 30 to 40 minutes longer. When pie is about half done, take a knife and push top apples down to soften. Continue to bake until done.

*Laura Brenneman*
*Morley, Michigan*

# Apple Dumplings

Dough:
2 C Flour
1/2 tsp. Salt
1/2 C Milk

2 1/2 Tsp. Baking Powder
2/3 C Shortening

Mix dry ingredients. Cut in butter. Add milk to make dough.

Sauce:
2 C Brown Sugar
1/4 C Butter
6 Apples, Peeled and Cut in halves.

2 C Water
1/2 tsp. Cinnamon

Roll out dough, cut in squares. Place one apple half on each square. Wet edges of dough and press into a ball around the apple. Set dumplings in a pan. Pour sauce over dumpling and bake. Bake at 350° for about 45 mins. or until lightly browned.

*Laura Brenneman*
*Morley, Michigan*

33

David Miller
Applecreek, Ohio
Age 8

# Apple Crisp

4 C Peeled and Sliced Apples
1 Tbsp. Lemon Juice
1/3 C Sifted Flour
1 C Oats

1/2 C Brown Sugar
1/2 tsp. Salt
1 tsp. Cinnamon
1/3 C Butter, Melted

Place apples in shallow baking dish. Sprinkle with lemon juice. Combine dry ingredients and add melted butter, mixing until crumbly. Sprinkle over apples and bake 30 minutes at 375°.

*Mrs. Orle Detweiler*
*Inola, Oklahoma*

# Apple Scotch Dessert

Syrup
1/4 C Brown Sugar
1 Tbsp. Cornstarch

2 C Water

Mix well and cook until bubbly. Cook and stir 2 more minutes. Then Add:
1 tsp. Vanilla

2 Tbsp. Butter

Remove from heat and pour into 13 x 9 in. pan. Combine the following:
2 C Flour
1 Tbsp. Baking Powder

1/4 C Sugar
more ingredients
on next page

Continued

Then Cut in:  1 C Shortening - as for dough.

Add 3 C Chopped, Peeled Apples and 1 C Milk (or enough to moisten).
Add in: 1/2 tsp. Vanilla.  Put apple dough mixture over syrup in pan, with a tablespoon.  Dot with butter.  Mix 1 Tbsp. Sugar, 1/2 tsp. Cinnamon and sprinkle over.  Bake in 350° oven for 50 to 55 minutes.  Serves 10.

*Lobelville, Tennessee*

# Saucy Apple Delight

Batter
| | |
|---|---|
| 1 C Flour | 1 tsp. Vanilla |
| 2 tsp. Baking Powder | 1/2 C Milk |
| 3/4 C Brown Sugar | 1 C Raisins |
| 2 Lg. Apples-Peeled & Shredded | 1/2 tsp. Salt |

Sauce
| | |
|---|---|
| 3/4 C Brown Sugar | 2 C Boiling Water |
| 1/4 tsp. Nutmeg | 1/2 tsp. Cinnamon |
| 2 Lg. Apples-Peeled & Shredded | 1/4 C Butter |

Combine batter ingredients; blend well.  Pour into greased 2 quart baking dish.  Sauce: Combine sugar, nutmeg, cinnamon, butter and boiling water.  Stir until butter is melted.  Add apples.  Pour over batter - DO NOT STIR - sauce floats on top. As the pudding bakes, the sauce seeps to bottom.  Bake uncovered at 375° for 30 minutes.  Serve warm, plain or with whipped cream or ice cream.

*Edith Miller*
*Kalona, Iowa*

# Cranberry Apple Crisp

3 C Chopped Peeled Baking Apples
2 C Fresh or Frozen Cranberries
1 C Sugar
3 Tbsp. All Purpose Flour

Topping:
1 1/2 C Quick Cooking Oats     1/2 C All Purpose Flour
1/2 C Packed Brown Sugar     1/4 C Chopped Pecans
1/2 C Butter or Margarine (Melted)

Combine apples, cranberries, sugar and flour - pour into greased 11 x 7 x 2 in. baking dish. In a bowl mix topping ingredients until crumbly; sprinkle over apple mixture. Bake at 350° for 50 to 55 minutes or until the fruit is tender. Yield: 6 to 8 servings.

*Sadie C. Brenneman*
*Morley, Michigan*

# Sour Cream Apple Pie

1 Egg Beaten
1 1/2 C Sugar
1/2 tsp. Cinnamon
1/2 C Brown Sugar
2 Tbsp. Butter

1 C Sour Cream
2 Tbsp. Flour (rounded)
4 C diced apples
1 Tbsp. Flour

Mix egg, sour cream, sugar, 2 tablespoons flour and cinnamon. Into this mix the apples. Pour into unbaked 9 in. pie shell. Combine brown sugar, 1 tablespoon flour and butter until crumbly. Cover top with crumbs and bake at 400° till apples are soft and crust is brown.

*Alta C. Schlabach*
*Millersburg, Ohio*

# Apple Gurnt

1/2 C Sugar
1 C Flour
1/2 tsp. Soda
1/2 C Sour Milk or Buttermilk
1/2 tsp. Vanilla

2 Tbsp. Shortening
1/2 tsp. Salt
1 tsp. Baking Powder
1 1/2 C Sliced Apples

Crumbs
6 Tbsp. Brown Sugar
1 1/2 tsp. Flour

1 1/2 tsp. Cinnamon

Cream sugar and shortening. Add egg and beat. Add soda to buttermilk and add to mixture. Sift dry ingredients, and add, beating thoroughly. Add sliced apples and blend into mixture. Pour into a greased, shallow baking dish. Sprinkle crumbs on top. Bake at 375° for 35 to 40 minutes. Serve hot with milk.

# Dutch Apple Pudding

1 3/4 C Flour
4 Apples, Peeled and sliced
2 Tbsp. Sugar
1 Egg

1/2 tsp. Salt
2 tsp. Baking Powder
1 Tbsp. Butter
3/4 C Milk

Rub butter into flour. Beat egg and milk together. Add to flour mixture. Mix to a dough. Spread part of dough (1/2 in. thick) into greased baking pan. Put apples on top. Sprinkle with sugar. Put remaining dough on top. Pour sauce on top. Bake in 375° oven for 20 minutes. Serve with milk. Cont. P.40

Andrew Miller
Applecreek, Ohio
Age 9

# Sauce

1 C Brown Sugar
2 C Water

3 tsp. Cornstarch
1 Tbsp. Butter

Combine brown sugar and cornstarch, then add water. Boil 3 minutes. Stir in butter.

*Sarah Miller*
*Jeromesville, Ohio*

# Baked Apples

5 Large Apples
1/4 C Raisins or Chopped Nuts

1/2 C Brown Sugar
2 Tbsp. Butter

Wash and core apples. Fill the cores with the brown sugar, nuts and dot with butter. Place in baking dish or casserole and put enough water around them just to cover bottom of pan. Bake in oven at 350° for about one hour or until apples are tender and are easily pierced with a fork. When almost done baking, put a few miniature marshmallows on top, if desired.

*Sadie Brenneman*
*Morley, Michigan*

 # Apple Pie Bars

2 1/2 C Flour
3/4 tsp. Salt
6 Tbsp. Flour
2 Qt. Sliced Apples or
   Apple Pie Filling.

1 C Shortening
1 Egg, Separated
1 1/3 C Sugar

Continued

Mix flour, shortening, and salt together. Separate egg, putting yolk in measuring cup and add enough milk to make 2/3 cup. Mix with blended ingredients. Roll out 1/2 of pastry and place on cookie sheet. Cover with apples, then sprinkle with mixture of sugar, cinnamon, and 6 tablespoons flour over apples. Cover with remaining pastry. Beat egg white until foamy and brush over top of dough. Sprinkle with sugar. Bake at 425° for 10 minutes, then finish at 375° for 25 minutes.

*Mrs. Orie Detweiler*
*Inola, Oklahoma*

# *Applesauce Cake*

1 C Sugar (White or Brown)
1/2 C Shortening
1 Egg
1 C Sifted Flour
1/2 tsp. Salt
1/2 tsp. Baking Powder
1 C Applesauce

1 tsp. Soda
1/2 tsp. Cloves
1 tsp. Cinnamon
1 tsp. Allspice
1 C Raisins
1/4 C Chopped Nuts

Cream shortening. Add sugar, beat until light. Add egg and beat until fluffy; add applesauce and mix. Sift flour, salt, baking powder, soda, cloves, cinnamon and allspice together and add raisins and nuts. Combine the two mixtures.

Pour into greased and floured 9 x 13 in. pan. Bake in oven at 350° for 40 to 45 minutes.

*Lobelville, Tennessee*

# Chilled Apple-Graham Loaf

24 Graham Cracker Squares     1 C Applesauce
1 C Whipped Topping           3 Bananas

Place six graham crackers on cookie sheet or cake pan; spread with 1/3 cup applesauce. Slice one banana and arrange slices over applesauce. Repeat for two more layers. Top with graham crackers and frost with whipped topping. Refrigerate 4 to 6 hours. Slice and serve.

*Mrs. David Miller*
*Applecreek, Ohio*

# Shoestring Apple Pie

4 C Shredded Apples     2 Tbsp. Flour
2 C Sugar               Vanilla
3 Eggs                  Pinch of Salt
1/2 C Water             Cinnamon

Pour apples in unbaked pie crust and mix rest of ingredients, except cinnamon and pour over apples. Sprinkle with cinnamon. Bake at 350° for 45 minutes or until done.

*Mrs. Orie Detweiler*
*Inola, Oklahoma*

# Grandma Nora's Apple Pudding

2/3 C Sugar
1/2 tsp. Baking Powder
1/2 C Chopped Nuts
1 tsp. Vanilla

1/3 C Flour
1/8 tsp. Salt
1 Egg, Well Beaten
2 C Peeled and Grated
    Apples

Stir dry ingredients together two or three times.  Add well
beaten egg, vanilla, nuts and apples.  Pour into well buttered
8 in. square baking dish.  Bake at 375° oven for 30 minutes.
Serves 4 to 6.

*Laura Brenneman*
*Morley, Michigan*

# Raw Apple Pudding

Mix several cups diced apples, about 1/4 cup chocolate
shavings (or chips), nuts, broken graham crackers with
whipped cream.  Chill.

*Laura Brenneman*
*Morley, Michigan*

# Spiced Apple Dessert

4 Large Apples
  (Cubed or Sliced)
1 C Flour
1/2 tsp. Baking Powder
1 tsp. Cloves
4 Tbsp. Butter

1 C Brown Sugar
1 tsp. Cinnamon
1/2 tsp. Soda
1 tsp. Nutmeg
1/2 tsp. Salt
2 Eggs, Beaten

Put dry ingredients together then add apples, eggs and butter.
Bake 45 minutes at 350°. Eat with milk and sugar when cooled.

*Laura Brennenman*
*Morley, Michigan*

# Applesauce Cake

3/4 C Shortening
1 1/4 C Sugar
3 Eggs
1 C Brown Sugar
1 3/4 C Applesauce
1/2 C Water
3 C Sifted Flour

1/2 tsp. Baking Powder
1 3/4 tsp. Soda
1 1/4 tsp. Cinnamon
1/2 tsp. Cloves
3/4 tsp. Allspice
3/4 tsp. Nutmeg
1 3/4 tsp. Salt

Cream shortening and sugar. Add eggs. Then add applesauce
(sweetened) and water, stirring well after each addition. Sift
dry ingredients and add to mixture. Bake at 350° in a 13 x 9 in.
pan for 30-35 min. or until done in the middle.

*Sarah Miller*
*Jeromesville, Ohio*

Pleasant
View
School

Andrew Miller
Applecreek, Ohio
Age 9

# Delicious Apple Pie

2 C Water
2 C Sugar or Less
3 Heaping Tbsp. Clear Jell
    (thickened with cold water)

Pinch of Salt
2 Tbsp. Butter
2 tsp. Cinnamon
3-4 C Apple Slices

Bring all ingredients except apples to boil. Put apple slices in crust and pour juice over apples. Top with crust. Bake at 400° for one hour or until done.

*Laura V. Troyer*

# Blushing Apple Pie

Have Dough for 2 Crust Pie Ready

Filling:

1/2 C Sugar
3 Tbsp. Water
2 Tbsp. Corn Starch

1/3 C Cinnamon Candies
6 C Sliced Peeled Apples
1/4 tsp. Nutmeg

In a large saucepan combine sugar, candies and water. Simmer over low heat until candies are dissolved. Stirring occasionally. Stir in 2 cups of apple slices, cornstarch and nutmeg. Quickly fold remaining apples into mixture, stirring until slices are evenly coated. Work quickly so candy mixture does not harden before apples are coated. Spoon mixture into pie crust lined pan. Add top crust and bake in 400° oven.

*Edith Miller*
*Kalona, Iowa*

# Apple Bread Pudding

6 Slices Whole Wheat Bread
1/3 C Melted Butter
1/2 C Sugar
1/2 tsp. Cinnamon

2 C Applesauce
1/2 C Raisins
1/4 C Maple Syrup

Cut crusts from bread slices. Cut each into three strips. Roll strips in butter and then in sugar and cinnamon. Line bottom of baking dish with bread strips. Add half of the applesauce. Sprinkle with raisins. Repeat same, ending with bread strips. Pour syrup over all. Bake at 350° for about 30 minutes or until top is golden brown. Serve warm with whipped cream.

*Vernie Schwartz*
*Stanwood, Michigan*

# Apple Cake

6 Tbsp. Butter
2 C White Sugar
2 Eggs
2 C Flour
1 tsp. Nutmeg

2 tsp. Soda
2 tsp. Vanilla
1 tsp. Salt
1 C Nuts
6 C Chopped Apples

Cream butter and sugar together and beat in eggs one at a time. Add dry ingredients and mix well. Add apples and nuts and mix thoroughly. Bake in a greased 13 x 9 in. pan for 1 hour at 350°.

*Anna Marie Weaver*

David Miller
Applecreek, Ohio
Age 8

# SALADS!

## Fruit Salad

Dressing:
8 C Water                    1 1/2 C Sugar
6 oz. Lemon Jello

Thicken with 5 tablespoons of clear Jell.

Pour over:  Pineapple, Apples, Grapes, Oranges &
Marshmallows

*Carol Coblentz*
*Grandin, Missouri*

## Dressing for Apple Salad

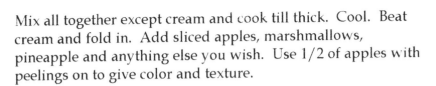

2 C juice from canned Pineapple   3/4 C Sugar
  (with added water)              1 Egg
2 Tbsp. Mira Clear                1 1/2 Tbsp. Butter
  or Cornstarch                   1 C Cream

Mix all together except cream and cook till thick.  Cool.  Beat
cream and fold in.  Add sliced apples, marshmallows,
pineapple and anything else you wish.  Use 1/2 of apples with
peelings on to give color and texture.

*Edith Miller*
*Kalona, Iowa*

# Red Hot Apple Salad

Put 1 1/4 cup water in a pan. Bring to boil. Add 1/4 cup Red Hot Cinnamon Candies. Cook until melted. Add one 3 oz. pkg. Red Jello. Chill. When it starts to jell, add 1 cup apple sauce. Crushed, drained pineapple may be added as well. Very good and easy!

*Edith Miller*
*Kalona, Iowa*

# Apple Cranberry Salad

1 C Sugar
1 C Cranberries

1 Orange - use 1/2 of peeling
5 Apples with peelings

Grind together and let set 2 hours. Make two 3 oz. boxes of strawberry jello according to directions. Mix all together when jello starts to thicken. Very good with turkey!

*Edith Miller*
*Kalona, Iowa*

# Cran-Apple Delight

3 C Chopped, Unpeeled Apples
2 C Cranberries (fresh or frozen)

Mix above ingredients and place in oblong baking dish.

Topping:

1 1/2 C Oatmeal
1/2 C Brown Sugar
1/2 C Chopped Pecans

1 Stick Melted Butter
1/3 C Flour

Mix well and spoon evenly over cranberries and apples. Bake at 350° for 45 minutes to an hour.

*Mrs. David Miller*
*Applecreek, Ohio*

 # Peanut Butter Apple Salad

1 1/2 Qt. Apples - Cubed
1/2 C Raisins
1/3 C Chopped Nuts - Optional

1 C Marshmallows
1/4 C Celery - Optional

Dressing:
1/2 C Salad Dressing
1/3 tsp. Salt
1/2 C Sugar

1/4 C Peanut Butter
1/2 Tsp. Maple Flavor
1/4 C Cream

Whip till well mixed. Pour over apples and serve.

*Carol Coblentz*
*Grandin, Missouri*

# Apple-Cabbage Slaw

Dressing:

2 tsp. Honey
1/2 tsp. Salt
1/2 tsp. Prepared Mustard
1 Tbsp. Vinegar
1/2 C Sour Cream or
   Plain Yogurt

2 C Sliced Apples
3 C Shredded Cabbage
1/2 tsp. Pepper (Optional)
1 1/2 tsp. Lemon Juice
   (Optional)

Mix sour cream or yogurt and seasonings. Sprinkle lemon juice over apples to prevent darkening. Mix apples and cabbage together. Pour dressing over mixture and toss lightly. Chill.

*Lobelville, Tennessee*

# Taffy Apple Salad

1 Tbsp. Flour
1 Egg
1-8 oz. Tub Whipped Topping
1-8 oz. Can Crushed Pineapple
   Drained - Reserve Juice

1/2 C Sugar
1 Tbsp. Vinegar
4 C Red Delicious Apples
   (Chopped)
1 C Dry Roasted Peanuts

Combine flour and sugar; beat egg and add to flour and sugar. Add vinegar and reserved pineapple juice. Cook over low heat in small saucepan. Cook until thick. Cool. Pour over apples, pineapple and peanuts, mix with whipped cream. Top with peanuts if desired.

*Mrs. Orie Detweiler*
*Inola, Oklahoma*

Mervin M. Miller
Applecreek, Ohio
Age 6

 # Meat-Apple Salad

1 C Cold Pork or Lunch Meat Chopped
2 Diced Apples
2/3 C Chopped Celery
1/4 C Pimentos
1 C Miracle Whip
Lettuce

Blend all ingredients except lettuce. Serve chilled on
sandwiches with lettuce and fresh tomato slices.

*Mrs. David Miller*
*Applecreek, Ohio*

# Apple Salad

1-20 oz. Can Crushed Pineapple
1-8 oz. Pkg. Cream Cheese
1 C Chopped Apples-Unpeeled
1 C Cool Whip
1-3 oz. Pkg. Lemon Jello
1 C Celery
1/2 C Nuts
2/3 C Sugar

Boil pineapple with juice and sugar for 3 minutes. Add dry
jello and stir well, let cool slightly. Add cream cheese and cool.
Add apples, celery and nuts. Add Cool Whip and spread in
pan to cool.

*Vernie Schwartz*
*Standwood, Michigan*

# Apple Salad

Dice apples, any amount you want.  Add crushed pineapple, miniature marshmallows, nuts and bananas - any amount you want.

Cook a sauce of 1 beaten egg, 1 cup sugar, 2 rounded tablespoons flour, 1 tablespoon vinegar and 1 pint water until it thickens.

Remove from heat and add butter size of walnut and 1 teaspoon of vanilla, cool and pour over fruit.

*Vernie Schwartz*
*Standwood, Michigan*

# Apple Jello Salad

1- 3 oz. Jello - any flavor          2 Apples - Thinly Sliced
                                       or Shredded.

Mix Jello according to directions and set aside till slightly thickened.  Peel apples and add to Jello.  Let thicken completely.  Very refreshing plain or you can put whipped topping on to serve.

*Mattie Yoder*
*Charm, Ohio*

*The Bible is to be bread for our daily use, not cake for special occasions.*

# Fruit Slaw

1-20 oz. can crushed
    pineapple, well drained
8 oz. Soft Cream Cheese
1/2 C Chopped Walnuts

3 C Shredded Cabbage
1 C Chopped Celery
1 C Chopped Apple

Combine pineapple and cream cheese - mix until well blended.
Add remaining ingredients. Toss lightly. Chill and enjoy.

*Kathryn Hostetler*
*West Farmington, Ohio*

# Apple Carrot Salad

## Sauce

Juice of 20 oz. can Pineapple
1 Tbsp. Flour

1/2 C Sugar
more ingredients
in directions

Cook together until thick. Add 1 beaten egg, cook 1 minute
longer. When cold, fold in 1 Cup whipping cream, whipped or
2 Cups frozen whipped topping.

Then peel and chop 3 apples. Grate 2 medium size carrots.
Mix with sauce and chill. You can also add raisins.

*Sara Hostetler*
*W. Farmington, Ohio*

# Jelled Fruit Salad

1-8 1/4 Oz. Can Crushed
  Pineapple
Cold Water
1 Med. Chopped Apple

1 - 3 Oz. Lemon Jello
1 C Boiling Water
8 Oz. Cream Cheese (Soft)

Drain pineapple - reserve syrup.  Dissolve Jello in boiling
water, add syrup and enough cold water to measure 1/2 Cup.
Gradually add to cream cheese.  Mix until well blended.  When
partially set, fold in fruit.  Pour into 8 in. square baking dish.
Chill until firm.

*Kathryn Hostetler*
*W. Farmington, Ohio*

# Amish Waldorf Salad

1 8 Oz. Cream Cheese
1 Tbsp. Orange Rind - grated
3 C Chopped Apples
1/2 C Chopped Pecans.

2 Tbsp. Orange Juice
1 Tbsp. Sugar
1 C Chopped Celery

Combine softened cream cheese, orange juice and rind.  Add
sugar - mix until well blended.  Then mix with other
ingredients.  Chill.  Serves 8.

*Kathryn Hostetler*
*W. Farmington, Ohio*

# *Fruit Dip*

1 Small Container Strawberry Yogurt
2 Tbsp. Marshmallow Cream
2 Tbsp. Cool Whip

Mix and serve with sliced fruit.

*Kathryn Hostetler*
*W. Farmington, Ohio*

 ## *Raw Apple Salad*

| | |
|---|---|
| 1/2 C Water | 1/2 C Sugar |
| 1 Tbsp. Flour | Pinch of Salt |
| 1 Beaten Egg | 2 tsp. Vinegar |
| Butter | 4 Apples |

Mix all ingredients together and boil for 1 minute. Add butter, size of an egg and cool. Peel and dice 4 apples and toss with sauce.

*Sara Hostetler*
*W. Farmington, Ohio*

## BREADS, ROLLS, ETC!. . . . . . . . . . . . . . . . . . . . .  1

DELICIOUS APPLE ROLLS..................................1
APPLE DOUGHNUTS ....................................1
APPLESAUCE MUFFINS ...................................2
APPLE-CINNAMON WAFFLES ...........................2
APPLE ROLLS ...............................................3
APPLE BREAD ...............................................4
APPLE BREAD ...............................................4
APPLE DIP....................................................5
APPLE DANISH .............................................5
APPLE ROLLS................................................6
APPLE PANCAKES..........................................7
RED APPLE RINGS..........................................7

## COOKIES ...............................................  8
DICED APPLE COOKIES....................................8
APPLE BARS................................................10
APPLE COOKIES...........................................10
FRESH APPLE BARS.......................................11
GLAZED APPLE COOKIES ...............................12
APPLE CHIP COOKIES....................................13
SPICY APPLE SQUARES..................................14
APPLESAUCE COOKIES...................................14
EASY APPLE FILLED COOKIES..........................15
APPLE BARS................................................16
SUGARLESS FRUIT COOKIES ...........................18
APPLE OATMEAL COOKIES..............................19

## DESSERTS! ...........................................  20
SPICED APPLE DESSERT..................................20
CHOCOLATE CHIP APPLESAUCE CAKE.................20
STEAMED APPLE PUDDING..............................22
APPLE GOODIE ...........................................23
APPLE CAKE................................................24

BAKED APPLES.................. 24
CARAMEL DIP FOR APPLES ..................... 26
APPLE FRITTERS.................. 26
BUTTERY CINNAMON APPLES................. 27
APPLE FRITTERS.................. 27
APPLE TORTE .................. 28
ROMAN APPLE CAKE................. 28
APPLE CRUNCH ................. 29
APPLE CRISP DESSERT................. 29
FRENCH APPLE PIE................. 31
APPLE BREAD.................. 31
APPLE CRISP.................. 32
COCONUT APPLE PIE................. 32
APPLE CREAM PIE................. 33
APPLE DUMPLINGS ................. 33
APPLE CRISP.................. 35
APPLE SCOTCH DESSERT................. 35
SAUCY APPLE DELIGHT.................. 36
CRANBERRY APPLE CRISP.................37
SOUR CREAM APPLE PIE.................. 37
APPLE GURNT .................. 38
DUTCH APPLE PUDDING ................. 38
BAKED APPLES.................. 40
APPLE PIE BARS.................. 40
APPLESAUCE CAKE.................. 41
CHILLED APPLE-GRAHAM LOAF ................. 42
SHOESTRING APPLE PIE.................. 42
GRANDMA NORA'S APPLE PUDDING ................. 43
RAW APPLE PUDDING ................. 43
SPICED APPLE DESSERT.................. 44
APPLESAUCE CAKE.................. 44
DELICIOUS APPLE PIE.................. 46
BLUSHING APPLE PIE.................. 46
APPLE BREAD PUDDING ................. 47
APPLE CAKE.................. 47

## SALADS! ... 49

FRUIT SALAD ... 49
DRESSING FOR APPLE SALAD ... 49
RED HOT APPLE SALAD ... 50
APPLE CRANBERRY SALAD ... 50
CRAN-APPLE DELIGHT ... 51
PEANUT BUTTER APPLE SALAD ... 51
APPLE-CABBAGE SLAW ... 52
TAFFY APPLE SALAD ... 52
MEAT-APPLE SALAD ... 54
APPLE SALAD ... 54
APPLE SALAD ... 55
APPLE JELLO SALAD ... 55
FRUIT SLAW ... 56
APPLE CARROT SALAD ... 56
JELLED FRUIT SALAD ... 57
AMISH WALDORF SALAD ... 57
FRUIT DIP ... 58
RAW APPLE SALAD ... 58

# ORDERING INFORMATION

The Amish Way Cookbook . . . . . . . . . . . . . . . . . . . . . . . . . . . . . $12.95
200 Pages of authentic Amish recipes.

The Amish Recipe Sampler . . . . . . . . . . . . . . . . . . . . . . . . . . . . $ 4.95
A sampling of Amish cooking with sampler sayings.

An Amish Potpourri Cookbook . . . . . . . . . . . . . . . . . . . . . . . . . $12.95
Over 300 delicious recipes plus Amish poems. 170 pages.

Canning The Amish Way . . . . . . . . . . . . . . . . . . . . . . . . . . . . . . $ 6.95
A cook's collection of easy canning recipes. 89 pages.

Plain & Fancy Amish Cookie Recipes . . . . . . . . . . . . . . . . . . . . . $ 6.95
120 cookie and candy recipes! A great collection.

Apple Treats from Amish Country . . . . . . . . . . . . . . . . . . . . . . . $ 6.95
Delicious apple recipes from Amish kitchens plus drawings
by Amish children.

Katie's Dream Storybook ages 4-11. . . . . . . . . . . . . . . . . . . . . . . $ 5.95
The story of a little Amish girl and her customs.

Please include $1.75 postage for first book ordered and $1.00 for each
additional book. Send check or money order to:

Jupiter Press
77 So. Franklin Street
Chagrin Falls, OH 44022
PHONE: 1-440-247-3616   FAX: 1-440-247-5431